Passive Income:

How to Achieve Multiple Streams of Income, Gain Financial Freedom, and Make Money While You Sleep

By Brandon Blake

© **_Copyright 2016 - All rights reserved._**

In no way is it legal to reproduce, duplicate, or transmit any part of this document in either electronic means or in printed format. Recording of this publication is strictly prohibited and any storage of this document is not allowed unless with written permission from the publisher. All rights reserved.

The information provided herein is stated to be truthful and consistent, in that any liability, in terms of inattention or otherwise, by any usage or abuse of any policies, processes, or directions contained within is the solitary and utter responsibility of the recipient reader. Under no circumstances will any legal responsibility or blame be held against the publisher for any reparation, damages, or monetary loss due to the information herein, either directly or indirectly.
Respective authors own all copyrights not held by the publisher.

Legal Notice:

This book is copyright protected. This is only for personal use. You cannot amend, distribute, sell, use, quote or paraphrase any part or the content within this book without the consent of the author or copyright owner. Legal action will be pursued if this is breached.

Disclaimer Notice:

Please note the information contained within this document is for educational and entertainment purposes only. Every attempt has been made to provide accurate, up to date and reliable complete information. No warranties of any kind are expressed or implied. Readers acknowledge that the author is not engaging in the rendering of legal, financial, medical or professional advice.

By reading this document, the reader agrees that under no circumstances are we responsible for any losses, direct or indirect, which are incurred as a result of the use of information contained within this document, including, but not limited to; errors, omissions, or inaccuracies.

Table of Contents

Introduction 1

Chapter 1: What Is Passive Income? 2

Chapter 2: Types of Passive Income 5

Chapter 3: How Can Passive Income Work for Me? 10

Chapter 4: What Are the Negative Aspects of Passive Income?
.... 15

Chapter 5: Organizing Your Time Effectively to Manage Your Passive Income Streams 20

Chapter 6: FBA (Fulfillment by Amazon) 25

Chapter 7: Kindle Publishing 30

Chapter 8: Affiliate Marketing 35

Chapter 9: Team up with a Partner to Accelerate Your Income
.... 39

Conclusion 45

By reading this document, the reader agrees that under no circumstances are we responsible for any losses, direct or indirect, which are incurred as a result of the use of information contained within this document, including, but not limited to; errors, omissions, or inaccuracies.

Table of Contents

Introduction 1

Chapter 1: What Is Passive Income? 2

Chapter 2: Types of Passive Income 5

Chapter 3: How Can Passive Income Work for Me? 10

Chapter 4: What Are the Negative Aspects of Passive Income? 15

Chapter 5: Organizing Your Time Effectively to Manage Your Passive Income Streams 20

Chapter 6: FBA (Fulfillment by Amazon) 25

Chapter 7: Kindle Publishing 30

Chapter 8: Affiliate Marketing 35

Chapter 9: Team up with a Partner to Accelerate Your Income 39

Conclusion 45

Introduction

In society today, we all seem to be working and sleeping and not achieving much more than this, at times. Sometimes you see people around you who seem to have more time, more money and even a nicer lifestyle than you. How do they do this you may ask yourself? Are they from a more well off family? The answer to these questions is probably "no," but I bet that most of them have some form of passive income, coming into them though.

So, what is passive income and how can it work for you? Well, this is something I am going to help you with for the duration of this book, so keep reading and I will show you what you can do to be one of "those" people. Yes, one who may also enjoy a better life, at least on a financial level. I will be honest and tell you now: passive income needs some investment, there may be risks involved, it does take up time, and there may be extra work needed on your behalf. However, if you do things right and become constantly aware, then the road to a more comfortable lifestyle can be coming your way, much sooner than you even thought possible. This book will help and guide you, so that you may have the knowledge to know just how you can make your own income, decisions, and choices when considering passive income as a long term earner for you.

Chapter 1: What Is Passive Income?

So, what exactly is passive income? Many people incorrectly assume that passive income means that there is never going to be any real work involved on their part. This isn't completely accurate. And let's be honest, no true investment is super easy. The IRS defines passive income as the, "net rental income and income from a business in which the taxpayer does not materially participate."

So, when you are earning a passive income, it means that you are going to be getting paid whether you actually do any meaningful work, or not. However, it doesn't mean that you never do any work, though. There can be a lot of work that needs to be done 'up front,' in order to get the ball rolling. Once that happens, it is a process of ongoing management. This is executed in an organized way, so that the workload is very manageable and also successful.

Alright, so there are some other things about passive income that you should know about in order to clear up any misconceptions you might have. This is important for your own understanding, from a law necessity view point.

Passive income is not: a one-time lump sum (like an inheritance), a form of permanent income, 100% secure, or always completely maintenance free.

Passive income is: a source of revenue with some continuity or an income that can eventually come to an end for various reasons.

I would like to share a personal tip of how things can be improved, even with all your new knowledge given in this book. This idea is called a "mastermind group." It is not a new idea, but for budding entrepreneurs like yourself, it is not quite readily spoken about enough.

A mastermind group or peer to peer accountability, is where a group of like-minded people talk with each other, who have the same goals for business or within a topic area. They offer mutual support, during times when maybe your income streams are slow, and they can advise on why and what to do, exponentially. They can also offer different perspectives, sometimes you might be looking too hard for an answer, and cannot see the obvious.

They can offer a wealth of knowledge on resources, and maybe they know good artists or they might know where to purchase items for the best prices. The group holds each other accountable, even though there is no connection from the business side. Additionally, everybody pushes each other (to not just reach their goals), but to surpass them, where possible.

How Do I Start a Mastermind group?

Pick topics that are related, agree on ground rules that relate to everybody. Pick your group partners. These should be "mutual beneficiaries" - not only can you benefit from them, but you can offer something to them. They should have a similar drive, and they should be problem solvers and have diverse skills that can be useful.

These groups should consist of 3-5 people, and have a set length of time to cater everyone. The meetings should have an agenda, someone to take notes and finally someone to lead the meeting.

It must be noted, these meetings do not actually have to take place face to face, they can be group chats over the internet.

Not only can these groups give motivation and assistance, they are a great way to expand your network. Make sure you learn and have fun!

Chapter 2: Types of Passive Income

With the following examples below, you will notice that these take the broader example of what people think of as passive income. These are primarily the gains on rentals, stocks, interest, retirement pay, lottery winnings, online work, and capital gains. It is important to remember to always check your tax implications with whatever option you decide to undertake. Be aware that passive income is taxable, exponentially. Check the amounts taxable in your area or location, so you are sure.

Dividend Stocks

This method is tried and tested over many years and can take little physical effort, except from a lot of research in finding stocks. This form of passive income can take a large investment initially, but if you continually invest smaller amounts, you could build a nice income over time. Note: stocks can go down as well as up. There is some risk involved with dividend stocks.

Rental Properties/Crowd Funding

There are a couple of options for this one. If you own a property and are not able to manage it by yourself, you can do this through a management company who normally charge a small percentage. The crowd funding or real estate investment trust approach is even more passive than just renting out a property, because all of the fundamental activity is managed by the company. Therefore, no activity is required by you, and all this one takes to start is your initial investment and then your money can start working for you without any intervention needed.

Peer to Peer Lending

This can be done through lending platforms like *Lending Club* and *Prosper*, which are set up to lend money to people that do not qualify for bank loans etc. Although there is a risk, the amount of investment can be small and you also have the choice of which lenders you want to help. Also, the good thing with this format is: the borrowers repay the initial capital plus interest at the same time, so your money is returned back to you, quicker. This leads to a faster turnaround for your cash, which leads to a greater return, minus the small management charges, that the website charges for these services.

Sell an eBook Online (self-publishing)

This is one of the most common forms of what is regarded as passive income today. To do this you just need a good idea or some research to find what topics people are reading at that moment. Most people tend to think that writing a book is outside of their capability or talent. Once you have your concept, you can outsource the writing and production of your book to an individual, or even a company, and then just have it uploaded to Amazon or another platform. After this, you just need to self-promote your book to build up interest, and hopefully you can build up steady sales. With this, the potential is there to publish many books over time, so you have a greater chance of success within this enormous market. There is some homework and research needed with this form of income, though.

Udemy

This is an online platform that sells video courses if you have a certain skill you can produce to create a video course of your own. Current figures suggest there are over 12 million people who use Udemy, so there will always be somebody who is looking to learn the skills that you possess. So, what can you teach someone? Your expertise can make you some great cash within the right niches on this educational platform. Check it out and see what you think, you may be a great teacher!

Blogs

Another popular way to earn a passive income is to write a blog and have affiliate links connected to it. As with your eBook, you will need a good concept in a niche market that is not oversaturated. With your blog you can concentrate on writing content that people want to read, then you have the potential to sell any number of products from your affiliates. If your blog is too general, there is a good chance it will not be noticed. Try to choose a niche range that is quite specific. As with self-publishing, you can outsource the design of your blog, and also your content writing if required. It is also possible to purchase an old blog that is no longer really used or maintained, and this can save time and money as most of the hard work has already been done.

Online Work

Although not as passive as most other options, it has to be mentioned. These days there are many websites that offer outsourcing of work for many different skills. If you have skills that you can offer people and some spare time, then the potential is there. Additionally, a lot of people have already managed to turn this path of earning into a full-time career. If choosing this route, time has to be given to building up a work reputation so you have the chance for repeat work. Sites are available online, so take the time to have a look around.

Become a Silent Partner

If you have the capital and know of a business that requires capital for expansion, you can become a silent partner. Instead of just offering the loan and receiving repayments, you could take an equity stake in the business, as well. From there, all the day to day operations are handled by the business owner, while you as a silent partner just receive a percentage of the profits.

Now you have a good guide to what is achievable, depending on your circumstances either financially or for the time you are able to commit. Many of the examples given can be utilized to work together. The possibilities are endless and are only really limited by your imagination and business sense, fundamentally. Just always do your research first and the rest will follow on positively from there. Time management can also be beneficial when you enter the passive income 'world.' If you manage your time properly, you will be able to incorporate more than one passive earning income type, or alternatively, just focus wholly on one important one.

Chapter 3: How Can Passive Income Work for Me?

There are a couple of different ways that a passive income can work for you, and there are many who think that having a passive income is a secondary return on their investment. Some people believe it will add to and increase their monetary funds for the future. These people are the ones who are either in a position of not working e.g. retired, or they have normal jobs and just want that little bit extra at the end of the month. On the other side of the coin, so to speak, are the ones who have realized that there is a real opportunity to turn something they are either passionate about into something amazing. They also believe that there is a possibility that they can have a career change and become self-sufficient from there enterprises.

If you take a traditional approach to your savings or pension, this would be deposited in the bank and you would get a rate of interest. As we all know, the only benefit is in the latter years when the amount of money in your account has increased in size, over time. Also with this example, you are under the control of the banks or the investment company, and you have no control about it apart from changing accounts or choosing the terms given etc.

If you take the passive income approach, your earning potential can be greatly increased, especially if you are linked to affiliate programs or have eBooks. This is because you have the chance to earn from your projects 24 hours per day and 7 days per week. Now to me, that sounds like a better option and a better way to use your money. If you plan your strategy wisely, you have one point of focus that gives you multiple revenue streams, as well.

To make you more aware of the possibilities I will give you an example of how things can be linked and work together for the benefit of your projected passive income projects:

Decide on Your Niche Market – What is your main focus area?

Create a Blog - If you have no skills, outsource the design.

Write Interesting Content - Find the correct person, this can be outsourced if needed.

Join Affiliate Programs - Amazon is the biggest name, with commission on sales.

Join Advertising Programs - Google AdSense, with commission on sales.

You just need to attract enough traffic to your blog, after the ads and the links to Amazon can be tailored to the nature of your blog. So, every time there is a purchase by someone following your link you get a monetary commission. All this can be done without too much intervention by yourself because you can have your blog updates outsourced, or you can be actively involved with the content on your blog. If you have another idea for a blog, you can create a second one and get double the exposure for advertising possibilities. Additionally, some people create multiple websites or blogs, just to take advantage of this form of passive income.

It is also possible to go even further, if you publish your own eBooks. These can be advertised and sold, and from here you can create podcasts to create interest; the possibilities are endless. Also, now you have exposure to the whole global online community who are potential customers, so you can create an email list with extra content and maybe even special offers. This gains more exposure and more potential customers. When you compare that to the money you have just sitting in a savings account, there really is no comparison.

If passive income is a new venture for you, it will probably mean you are still working at this time. So, hopefully you can use some of that money to build up your investment finances for another passive income ventures, where possible.

There is another way to look at passive income and this is known as *Jobs vs. Passive Income,* so let me explain.

We all know everyone needs a job, but does it really have to be a normal job? A 9 -5 job used to mean security for now and for the future, but not anymore. How many people actually have a job they really enjoy which gives them lots of free time and financial security? You do a full day's work and get a set rate, that will be the same (usually without increase), and only ever changing if you have a pay rise, or change job roles for a higher pay rate.

The best way to express the meaning of passive income is to say, earning money from one-time work.

At the time of inception (of your ideas and initial setup), the chance to grow only gets larger, if you decide to write an eBook, it may take many, countless hours, but once those hours are over, you still have the chance to earn multiple times over, as long as your book has the potential to sell well. You can increase this through promotions or email lists, too.

Other ways to compare passive income to 'normal' jobs:

With a normal job you are working for someone else, so you will have fixed working hours. There will only be certain times of the year when you can take a vacation. You will find that within your normal job you may also pay a higher tax rate. Companies can close and people can get made redundant, so you have to start the whole process again, if this occurs. You will need to look for a job and then compete to find a job that is suitable - and once again try to work your way up through the ranks, if it is within a corporate or business setting.

If you are lucky and you have a job for the rest of your working life, you only have the chance to retire at the age denoted by the government. But, with a successful passive income, you have the potential to retire at whatever age you decide is warranted. That's a big plus.

Having a passive income not only gives you the chance to work when you want (you still need to do some work), but it gives you the freedom to choose where you work, and what work you want to do. You can choose to work every day, every afternoon or just a few days a week, the choice is just up to you. There is much freedom gained through the passive income earning route. You can work as little, or as much as you want! This is the wonderful bonus of deciding to be a passive income earner, actually. So think on this...

Summary of How Passive Income Can Work for You:

- It can give a steady source of income
- It allows more free time to create more passive income ventures
- It can help an individual to reach financial freedom
- It can create unlimited success over time

Chapter 4: What Are the Negative Aspects of Passive Income?

Like everything in life, there are always downsides. So, earning a passive income is no exception. I will describe the negative points of traveling the passive income route, so you can be aware of some of the aspects that may come across your path.

Success Not Guaranteed

The major thing people forget when trying to earn a passive income is that success is not guaranteed, and overnight success is just a myth. It doesn't matter how hard you try or how much research you have done, there is no guarantee you will succeed. You can spend months creating an 'all singing all dancing' blog, only to have it fail due to the niche market you have chosen (e.g. not being a topic that people have taken to). If you fail, you should try to create alternative revenue streams, or maybe an alternative blog with a different topic whilst still pushing the one that has not been accepted…yet.

Social Life and Attention

If all this is new to you, it could take a while for you to adapt to a normal working environment, you may miss having your co-workers around you and the constant contact with other people. A little extra effort will be needed to make sure you go out to be social, especially at the start of your venture. Some other businesses I mentioned also require a lot of attention (examples being property rentals). And on paper, it seems like an easy job, but repairs on a property and finding the right tenants can really take its toll. Be mindful of these factors, here.

Low Income and Time Consumption

These are probably the main reasons that people quit when trying to earn a passive income. Until your revenue streams take hold and start earning an income, the return will be low and it will seem as if nothing is happening. For your business to provide a sustainable income, there will have to be a lot of effort and a lot of hard work done by you, or by the people you outsource to. The hours you work could be well over what you would work in a normal job. Lastly, depending on the niche you are in it could take up to 12 months before you start to see any profit at all.

Start Up Capital and Losing Money

With the amount of startup time required to see a return, the potential to actually lose money at the start can be both heartbreaking and soul destroying, at times. If your revenue streams are actually starting to generate some revenue - this will seem bearable, but if you are at a very early stage in your venture it will give you cause for worry. I recommend that before you start, it is worth checking all of your facts and figures to make sure you have enough capital to carry your venture through the first six months (without any gains). Depending on which venture/s you take, this may not be a massive amount of money. It could be something as simple as web hosting charges or something more substantial like building repairs or renovations, if we use the rental property market, as an example.

Customer Loyalty

One thing that is often overlooked is customer loyalty, this is something that you cannot do passively. Each customer expects to be cared for, and if they feel they are being neglected, there is a good chance they may go elsewhere. Without customers you have nothing. So if your passive income venture is customer based, be well aware of the x-factor for increasing and maintaining the customer based loyalty.

Keeping Up with Trends

Due to the fast pace of things in our modern world today, you have to pay close attention to changes, it is not possible to just sit back and wait for the money to come in. New developments or ideas are constantly being released which could leave your customers jumping ship, if your product lines are not 'hip' or keeping up with the current trends. In the property rental market, the look of your rental is key here too. Outdated kitchens or paint colors on the exterior or exterior of a property can have negative connotations to your earnings. So, keep up with the trends for your passive income venture/s.

Outsourcing and Teamwork

For whatever avenue you decide to take, there is a chance that a portion of it can be outsourced. Although this can save time and be a cheaper option, it is critical you find the right people to join your team. You may have freelancers who claim they can build websites for example, but after project completion, it is found that there are things they could not do, fundamentally. Your only solution for this would be to seek another party to correct the problems, or if you have rental properties and need workmen, they may not complete the work as promised. Apart from these team members you must be in a position to manage them correctly, and to give them guidance, and this takes time. A growing business of this nature cannot run itself without a good leader. If you outsource the majority of your projects - and you are not there at each step of the process, it is possible that the person (or people) you have entrusted work to, may not meet your needs or requirements, without your lead.

Complacency

There are other thoughts that challenge passive income, in that it creates a false or temporary sense of success which can lead to some complacency. The whole philosophy of passive income is not to just create one avenue stream, but to continue creating others which inspire you to add a value and extra finances to your working life as a whole. So, try to remain focused, because all great income streams need management, on a regular basis.

Being a Boss and Paying Tax

If you are on your way to packing in your 9 – 5 job and following your passive income endeavors, there is something that should not be overlooked. Firstly, you will now be a boss and you have to make all the decisions - and I mean *all,* and there will be no one above you to take responsibility or take liability. Actually, this stops with you! Then there is the tax man, and if you are generating enough revenue, your taxes will have to be paid. This should not be overlooked as just something that can be taken care of later.

At the end of the day, I still believe the advantages of earning a passive income outweigh the disadvantages most of the time, although there are some people who are just not the type to have this sort of lifestyle change. You need to be fully committed, because nothing comes for free. Work as hard as you can, and balance it out with stress management and relaxation. You really can do this, you know!

Chapter 5: Organizing Your Time Effectively to Manage Your Passive Income Streams

Having got this far, you must be considering going down the passive income route with your new idea or concept. So, after all the points I have highlighted previously, there is one thing that has not been mentioned - time management.

No one expects you to be running around like a headless chicken, or doing 100 hours a week and on your way to burnout before you have even started. You must have an achievable plan and you must allow time for yourself, because there is no fun when everything you do is work related.

Depending on the passive income revenue stream you venture in on, can determine how you allocate time. So then you can plan to manage your income streams effectively, and the basic principles will be the same. These techniques although not just geared to any income stream in particular, are good practices for effective time management. They can be adapted to whatever income streams you have now or plan on having in the future.

At the start of the day, take 30 minutes to plan the rest of your day and make sure nothing is done towards your business until you have completed your plan. By planning ahead of time, you will have a clear indication of what you need to achieve and what items or activities you need to accomplish as a priority.

Once you have your plan then you can create a daily schedule and carry it around with you; record thoughts, any conversations you may have regarding business, or personal activities. By doing this you will be able to see how much you can comfortably achieve on any given day, and where your time seems to have disappeared. Most importantly you will have a physical idea of what things you have not completed in that particular day, after reflection.

Any activity that is crucial to your business should have a time allocated to it, e.g. meeting rental manager 3-4pm. You should aim to keep these activities as close to the time you have allocated with no overruns, if possible. Not only will it enforce discipline, it will save wasting time that can be utilized for something else that is in your daily plan.

A lot of people use the practice of making a "things to do" list. Although this is alright for a quick reference – these lists have the habit of growing to the point they are unachievable. So incorporate them, over time so they do actually get done.

You can even create appointments with yourself on your schedule when you have specific tasks to do. E.g. 9am – 12 am update blog content or check emails, and by doing this you can see what time you have available, to accomplish other tasks. Sometimes it does take a little bit of self-discipline if you are working alone, but I promise you, once you are in the habit of doing it, you will not regret it.

When writing your plan for the day or your schedule, you should allocate at least 50% of your time on activities, conversations or thoughts on areas of your business that produce the best results. Doing this will help prioritize the important parts of your business, instead of spreading your energies in areas that are not as important.

Before every meeting, business phone call, or email, take a few minutes to decide what results you want to achieve, because this helps you to direct the correspondence in the direction you want - enabling you to achieve your desired goal before you start. If you did not manage to reach your desired goal, take a few minutes to determine what was missing and what else you could have done or said, and how you can use this the next time.

If you are working in a location where there are other people and you have important work to do, put a do not disturb sign up so they will not attract your attention. For unnecessary distractions, get into the habit of not just answering the phone when it is ringing, or answering an email just as it has been received. If people need your attention, they can wait a while until you are ready for them, because you are the one in control. Also, you have no obligation to keep jumping at every request. This being said, if it is crucial for your business that the interruption requires a personal response, then you should make the time to cater to them.

Unless your business is aimed towards social media to support your revenue streams, all social media should be turned off as these are a constant distraction.

Always remember it is nearly impossible to accomplish everything, by scheduling your time and yourself. Ideally, you will have a priority list that is easy to follow, and what needs to be completed, including what specific order.

Specialize in your niche, and in doing this you will have a central focus, and your ideas will not be spread across other topics. You will build up more knowledge and ideas and you will be more efficient at providing interesting content too, if that is part of your venture.

As a final solution to your time management, you may be becoming increasingly busy. Therefore, it is not possible for you to manage your time effectively while concentrating on your business. If this happens, you can hire a virtual assistant who can relieve you of some of your daily administration tasks, even if it is just for an hour or two per day. All your email responses, updating your diary and planning meetings can all be carried out by a VA. They can truly be irreplaceable when you get really busy.

Most aspects of your passive income can be carried out by a third party if you find you are too busy, and property rental management agents, content writing specialists, website technicians, and order processing VA's, can be outsourced.

Thus, giving you more chance to increase your business, and then your overall income.

Chapter 6: FBA (Fulfillment by Amazon)

There is a multitude of ways to earn money in the online market place, and I am going to explain the three most common ones at the moment. Although not just a list, I have compiled the informative process which outlines what you need to know.

Amazon Fulfilment Strategy

Amazon Fulfilment is a business strategy that allows you to send products to one of Amazon's warehouses, from here they will manage all picking and packing, shipping and finally customer service. Advantages for FBA range from more exposure to more customers and faster shipping. Here I will outline some informative steps to help you on your way.

Amazon Seller Account

Firstly, you need to create an Amazon seller account if you do not already have one. If you already have an Amazon account, then you can just add FBA as an option. Once you have signed up you will be given the choice of either an individual selling plan or a professional selling plan - which has a free month's trial. So, this can be useful as it will enable you to find out if this business type is actually for you, exponentially.

Research

As with most online businesses it is imperative to do your research, because what appears to be a good product to sell could actually be a slow mover. Also, not only will you be left with unwanted stock, but you could be liable for long term storage charges from Amazon, too. It is also worth noting that Amazon has many rules and procedures that should be followed. So read the fine print beforehand.

Products for Sale

There are many ways people find products to sell through Amazon, they either have access to manufacturing or they scout around purchasing items that are suitable for resale. The decisions of how you locate your products is yours. Additionally, you must do your research of what your business line will be, and what products you decide to sell. Whatever route you decide to take, it will cost you money, so you must be aware that there is a chance you could lose money if products are not sold.

Some places to locate deals are actually big retail stores, and here you can find many products at reduced prices, or items that are out of season which can be kept until a different time of year - when their price will be at a premium. Wherever you finally source your items, it is worth checking Amazon's sales rankings before you buy, this way you can see how quickly items of that nature are selling. I have noticed over time that the best form of items to make money on are bundles or multipacks. Sometimes these will eliminate competition from other sellers of single items of the same nature.

Product Listings

Once you have your range of products these must be entered into the Amazon catalog, and this can be done one at a time or it is possible to do it in bulk. Make sure your descriptions always include keywords that are searched by customers. E.g. Nike, EBook, Men's, Women's, or other important search engine optimized (SEO) words. Include colors, brand names, specifics and popular trending words, so that your items are found by buyers. This is fundamental.

Prepare your Products

Although it is Amazon who will do the picking and packing, you must ensure that all your products are "e-commerce ready", and this means they are ready to be shipped directly to your customer, both securely and safely. It is possible to have Amazon's preferred packaging shipped directly to you so you can pack your products in a specified way stipulated by Amazon, too.

Deliver to Amazon

When your goods are packed ready, you will then need to ship them to one of Amazon's warehouses which is closest to your location. This is usually carried out by one of Amazon's preferred carriers. So you will have track and tracing available to you - until your goods reach the fulfillment center of choice. Further information regarding this or other questions can be located on Amazon's online seller's tools web page.

Once Customer Has Ordered

Once an item has been ordered from Amazon and you have goods in stock, these will be picked and sorted ready for shipment. This service is fantastic really, because they do the work for you, here.

Customer Support

One of the main benefits of using FBA is the level of customer service that follows each sale. No matter where the customer is in the world, there is a customer support team available 24 hours per day, seven days per week. Amazing really.

Inventory and Accounts

It is worth setting up strict guidelines for yourself in this department as it can be quite easy to fail when something has been overlooked. The questions you need to ask yourself are: How are your accounts to be managed? How can you keep a check on your inventory? And who will do the sales and income tax, me or an accountant? These must be taken into consideration.

Other Peoples' Mistakes

It is a high possibility that at some point mistakes will be made, no matter who's fault it is. It is wise to keep your own eye on your stock without taking it for granted, it has been said that Amazon has lost stock for one reason or another. So be aware and plan on this, just in case.

Tools of the Trade

If you have decided to proceed as a business that you can see being worthwhile for you, there are a few tools that you may consider investing in which can help you to succeed. 1. Smartphone that can run a scanning app. 2. Laser labels (Avery is the best known brand). 3. Packaging tape and foam. 4. Easy to use bookkeeping application for finance and accounting management.

Things to Note

As previously mentioned, FBA is your business, you will be liable for taxes if you are earning enough, and you can hire an accountant to help. Check what pricing points are the fastest sellers, and try to find items in that price range. If buying new items, don't remove the manufacturers packaging, this will reduce the selling price. Compile a list of all the rules and regulations from Amazon - and keep it handy. Compile a list of all the charges that Amazon will charge so it will not come to you unexpectedly. If you purchase from a little or unknown retailer, be aware of fake or inferior items.

FBA can be very profitable if things are done right, although it is not always an easy option; you have to be smart. Trends keep changing, and there are always people that have better bargaining power tools than you. At the start, just concentrate on a few products, and don't try to become overwhelmed by the whole situation. Positive self-talk, dedication and organization are key factors, here.

Chapter 7: Kindle Publishing

The basic principle for Kindle Publishing (KDP) is quite a simple process, although there are guidelines set out by Amazon and other eBook sellers that must be followed. These basically consist of copyright, format, book title and description etc. As Amazon is the worldwide leader in eBook sales, I will aim to show you their guidelines. There is one other thing I should mention too, as the whole process is not as simple as having an idea for a book, then writing it and uploading it for selling. There are factors which need to be considered for effective success.

Sign up for an Amazon Account

If you go to the Amazon homepage, there is a heading at the bottom called "Make Money with Us."

In the list provided is a subheading "Self-Publish with Us," so you follow this link and it will take you to the "Create a Kindle Publishing Account" page. Here you can just follow the steps laid out by Amazon and create your account. The information required will consist of name, address, telephone number and the banking details for where your money shall be sent.

Book Content

If you have an idea or already written a book, that's all well and good, but there are a few things to consider. What niche is your book in and how much competition is there in this market? This is highly relevant as you can spend months on your idea just to find it is in a niche market that is over saturated. There are tips and tricks of how to analyze Amazon to find out what subjects are popular and in what niche.

If you have no book written it is advisable to research how to do this and then focus on that topic. Once you have researched and found an idea, you can either continue to write yourself, or find a site that can offer you to outsource the content writing.

Once written you must think of the cover (you can outsource this to an artist), and because the background on Amazon is colored white, strong bold colors are best which will stand out. The title should be large to enable it to read easily, too. A subheading must be chosen that should be descriptive and relevant to the book. These factors are important as they are included in the search fields when people are looking for purchases. With regards to formatting there are more guidelines, and the easiest and best way to understand this is to read it direct from the Amazon website, if you type, "Building Your Book for Kindle" into your browser search, you will find the link there, and it should be the first option available.

Time to Publish

Once all this is done and you are ready to publish, you can now go back to your Amazon account and proceed with the uploading of your new book. Amazon now allows many different file formats that you can upload with, and one of the most popular is *Microsoft Word* (stick with the simplest).

Once you have logged in to your *Amazon Kindle Account* you will arrive at your *Kindle Dashboard*, from here you can enter the following information and then be on your way to publishing your very own eBook.

Add your new book title – this must be the same as the title on the cover.

Enter the details of your book – there are many things you can enter here, but Amazon requires certain information. Book Name, Description, Book Contributors, Language, Verifying your Publishing Rights, Categories, Book Release Option, Digital Rights Management and of course your book file and cover file.

Uploading and Previewing Your Book

Upload your book as described on your Kindle page, (this is the much the same process as locating a file on your computer). Simply browse, find the file, and click open. At the same time, you are also given the chance to upload your wonderful book cover.

Once you have started to upload your book, it is automatically converted to Kindle during this process. Once uploaded the next page will show the online previewer. This is what your book will look like on different devices.

Verify Rights and Territories

In this section, you have to give some legal disclosure that you own the content and it has not been copied from any other source which is not just illegal but also unethical. As with the territories, it is advisable to select "Worldwide Rights," because this covers you around the globe and sets no limits on your potential customers.

Pricing and Royalty

Although you can charge any price you feel is right for your book, we have to revert back to the tips and tricks I mentioned at the start. Many people advise starting with a small selling price (as you are unknown) or if there is a lot of competition in this niche. Once your book starts attracting attention, you can always increase the price. Secondly, many kindle buyers search for books in certain price ranges, so check your options so as to give you the maximum exposure online.

Finally, you are asked what level of royalties you expect to receive. So, if your selling price is lower than $2.99 you will automatically receive the 35 percent royalty. The general amount that people set is 70 percent, although it is worth checking more on this as it can be affected by your upper-level price and book size.

Final Thoughts and Promotion

Once all that has been done, your book can go live in a matter of hours rather than days, and it is then your creation is on offer to everyone, although this is not necessarily enough to guarantee you sales. Amazon does have certain built-in options which help you promote. It is advisable to give exposure to your book on all social media platforms that you use, or if you have a blog or know someone who has a blog, you can link directly from there. It is also a great option to ask readers of your book to leave reviews, because this gives you exposure and helps you move up in the Amazon ranking system, which means more traffic to your cover.

Chapter 8: Affiliate Marketing

A brief description of affiliate marketing is "being affiliated with online stores," which basically means you are a salesperson for the stores and gain commission from any products customers buy when they have passed through you.

Research and Find That Niche Product

The first step to becoming an affiliate marketer is research, a lot of research. Many people choose something they are very passionate about or experienced in, because it enables them to constantly write entertaining, informative content that will attract possible customers. Although many people choose a niche that is close to their heart, it is also possible to find a niche that can be more profitable, and this may not be a topic or area where you have much experience. Even though this can be learned over time.

Choosing Affiliate Programs

After finding a niche that you consider to have enough potential for customers, you must not only research what products have affiliate programs, but also the amount of commission they offer from their products. Another thing to consider is, are the products you are promoting something that you, yourself would purchase? If you don't believe in your products - it will not only be hard to write about them, it will also be difficult to convince other people to buy them.

Another thing that is often overlooked by affiliate marketers when choosing an affiliate program is customer service. What support will that company provide in the case of faulty products and returns? Do you only get email replies or can you speak to someone directly, via chat or instant messaging? There is no doubt that support will be required somewhere along the line.

Website Time

Unless you already have a website or blog that is suitable for affiliate marketing, you will have to create one. Although building a website is much easier than it used to be, unless you have experience it can still be quite daunting. Fortunately, this is something you can outsource to be done, although you would have to pay for this service - it can save you a lot of time and effort to have it done correctly.

Secondly, with regard to your website, you also have to purchase a domain name and also set up website hosting. It's okay because all of this you can find and purchase while you are searching for your niche. It is recommended that you choose a decent hosting service even if they charge slightly more (as they can be more reliable in the future). With modern trends, it is highly possible you will come to use WordPress for your website, too. This is a content management system which makes it simple to keep your website updated and create and publish your content. It is important to consider at the design stage of your website the SEO (search engine optimization) word content. The more SEO used, the better. Think about this in all aspects of your website, because it is fundamentally important, overall.

Enriched Content, Traffic

This is one of the most important aspects that you need to give deep thought, because your content needs to be informative, engaging and of a standard that will encourage customers to re-visit your site. There is no chance of survival if you cannot offer this on a regular basis, and you need customers making return visits on a regular basis (and hopefully considering a purchase) while they are there.

The aim here is to drive as much traffic to the online retailer as is possible, by giving good product reviews, current trends, and new releases. You can create blog posts on current issues being spoken about your niche. As an example, if you already have an eBook - you can give this free or at a discount price if they make a purchase. A final tip is to promote your items in your blog posts rather than just in your advertising banner ads.

Link Building and SEO

You may be thinking, once I have visitors coming to my website how do I make money? Well, this is the importance of building links to your affiliates' online stores. Some people only put banner ads on their site, and from this they may get sales but you have many more options. If you have friends or know people with blogs, you can swap links. Google AdWords is a good option, although there may be a charge for this service. An email mailing list is a very good option, here you can mail most of your followers' news or updates along with special offers or discounts.

Other forms of viable link building strategies can be web directories, forum discussions, and social media. Here you need a long term linking plan, and it is much safer to use multiple sources. There is more exposure and it is also a safeguard if any of the methods you use fail, or the company goes out of business. One final method of creating links is to add a link to an image - which leads them direct to the sales page for that item. A few ways to optimize for SEO is to use meta tags, use search engine friendly URLs, repeat key phrases and finally you should "alt tag" your images. It is also possible to incorporate Pay Per Click (PPC) advertising, so for each click on your ads you will get paid - even if no purchase is made. And although this would only be a minor amount it can accumulate successfully, over time.

Get Educated

As a final note - there is never any good time to stop learning, so study your competition and what they are doing differently to you. You can study your products' good points and bad points, and most importantly their great selling points. Additionally, you can study customer reviews of similar products, and also study what you are doing yourself. Most affiliate programs offer some statistics reports, but it is worth doing your own analysis too, so you will know if you need to change your strategy and give yourself a better understanding of the process.

Chapter 9: Team up with a Partner to Accelerate Your Income

Although most people think creating passive income streams are created just for one person (with multiple revenue streams), there is also the possibility to have a mutual partnership. This can be with either a family member, a friend or a complete stranger! Whoever you have in mind to form this partnership with, there must be a few legal things that are required, and also a few ethical things that (although not required), should be thought about as you are building a successful partnership together.

Please Note

Not only do different countries have varying rules and regulations, but states in the US can have different rules and regulations also. The basic principles will be the same.

Partnership Agreement Outline

A partnership agreement will normally consist of paragraphs with spaces which need to be completed before it will become legal. I will explain what information can be required, and keep it as simple as possible. If it is just a mutual partnership you are forming, it is worth including the following sections.

Date

The agreement will stipulate the date the partnership starts, anything from this date must be done according to the agreement.

In Consideration of

Here the agreement will outline further details regarding the partnership.

Terms

Here the agreement will give a length of time that the partnership will run for, if there is no set time and one partner wishes to cease (for whatever reason), it will just state the agreement will run until ceased by one of the partners, and the way they can do this should be outlined elsewhere in the agreement.

Place of Business

This could be included if the partners have an actual location where they work from.

Partners

This will state the names of the partners that will be included.

Voluntary Withdrawal of Partner

This will outline how a partner should present, or that they wish to be no longer a part of the partnership. This is normally done in writing giving a specific notice period.

Involuntary Withdrawal of Partner

This will outline what needs to be done if one partner wishes to cease operating with the other. Reasons for this could be a breach of contract, unfair practices etc.

Dissolution

This would be when both partners decide to cease working together.

Accounts

Here there would be a section of how all the financials of the partnership would be handled, and also how a partner is able to withdraw the said funds.

Forbidden Acts

This could state the outlines of what is not accepted in the operation between the partners.

Liability

This would outline any liability that exists between the partners, either financial or if there is anything linked to the second partner's business, that the first partner is unaware of.

Witness and Partner Signatures

Here the agreement should be witnessed by two other people and then signed and dated by the partners. This is not a complete agreement, just an outline of some things that may be relevant to your situation, you should seek further legal advice before entering into any written agreement/s.

Always Communicate with Honesty

For the benefit of both sides, there should a level of transparency of communication between both partners. They must realize they are now representing two people and not just themselves. If working apart, it is better to have constant communication of how business is moving, this can be by telephone, text, instant messaging or email.

It would be counterproductive if either part was doing anything that could harm the partnership, it could also lead the partnership to be dissolved prematurely which could leave them losing financially, a part of the business. It could also have financial implications. One reason for honest communication is the fact that one partner could change, or commit to something regarding the business - and if the second partner is unaware (or it was done deceitfully), they could be in an embarrassing situation.

Handling Money

This is one of the most important aspects of forming a partnership, and the one thing that can cause arguments and confrontations. The partners should discuss how the finances should be controlled. This not only means any profits or royalty earned but also any money that is injected into the partnership, and how this can affect any percentage of the partner's entitlement. Especially if one partner has contributed a higher stake than the other.

It is possible for the partners to manage all the financials themselves, but due to business constraints this may not always be possible, and could lead to blame if anything goes wrong. It is highly advisable to seek the assistance of an external accountant who can advise, and also if needed do all the accounting, too. Including the book of accounts, tax payments and partners' entitlement (salaries).

Decision Making

The partners should discuss how any decision making should take place. If both parties hold an equal share of the partnership, neither side should make any decisions without consent from the other. If one party has a higher stake or control in the partnership, it could be agreed they are allowed to make choices without any confirmation to the other. Although from an ethical point of view, it is good practice to inform the other party if there are any decisions which need to be made.

Dividing Time

Dividing time equally between the two partners should be discussed early on, or before the partnership commences, even though things are likely to change throughout the course of the working life.

At the time of discussion, it is worth considering what each other's strengths and weaknesses are, and allocating jobs based on these to achieve the maximum benefits. For example, if one partner is good at content writing, they could do this, and if the other is good at creating traffic through social media, they could take charge of that task. If the time and tasks are divided that way, there should be updates passed to the second partner, of what has been accomplished. Then they have an instant overall picture of the state of the business.

Conclusion

I would like to thank you for purchasing this book, and really hope all the knowledge and insights I have tried to provide, can help you on your way to a financially rewarding business. I have written this with you in mind, and my passion comes from what I have gained from many successful years of having an amazing passive income stream.

Of course, I made mistakes, I learned from them too - and that is what I am passing on to you; knowledge and experience. Additionally, that is something you will not find on any list. Whilst writing this book for you, I relived many memories of how I started and where I am today. I feel proud it is something that I can pass on to you. As a final note, whichever road you travel in this exciting route to success and self-discovery, this is not the end. There are many paths to take, and there is no reason to settle for just one income stream...not only are multiple streams safer, but above all, you will be more successful, on the whole. So start small, and dream big, out into a larger expansion that allows you to grow, at your own pace. Live your life, be free!

www.ingramcontent.com/pod-product-compliance
Lightning Source LLC
Chambersburg PA
CBHW070414190526
45169CB00003B/1256